Antique Dol

AGNES MELGER

REBO
PRODUCTIONS

This book is dedicated to Wiebe Fokkema (Raymond Charrier)

© 1996 R&B, Lisse
© 1997 Published by Rebo Productions Ltd
Cover design: *Ton Wienbelt, The Netherlands*
Production: *TextCase, The Netherlands*
Translation: *Stephen Challacombe for First Edition Translations Ltd, Great Britain*
Typesetting: *Hof&Land Typografie, The Netherlands*

ISBN 1 901094 46 4

Contents

Foreword

With a degree of melancholy I look back on the pleasant years of childhood in spite of the hardship that the Second World War caused. There were scarcely any toys in those times. I just had a doll that my mother knitted for me from scraps of wool, which I cuddled until it was completely bald, and a little blue wooden kitchen that my father had put together with his own hands and with much love and patience for my sixth birthday. My first encounter with antique dolls was several years later, when, with my mother, I visited one of her aunts who lived in a fine house, where on a plush red sofa in the drawing room a group of beautiful dolls was seated. From the moment that they gazed at me with their brilliant, great glass eyes in their delicate china faces, they entranced me completely. The subconscious desire to possess such a doll must have lain dormant within me for a very long time until many years later, in a shop full of old knickknacks, I saw two doll's feet sticking out of a box, which on closer inspection proved to belong to a splendid doll by Armand Marseille. The doll had a pretty porcelain face and was made at the turn of the century. With a determination to collect old dolls, I went home with this doll, quite unaware of the fact that virtually all my spare time would be filled for the next twenty years as a result of my purchase. Together with my husband, who does not find collecting dolls as fascinating as I do, I have lost myself in the wide range of reading material, we have visited museums and seen many very interesting private collections. In short, we discovered a world created by children's play over the centuries. It would take more than one book to give a full overview of the history of the doll. Even so, I would like to make an attempt to share with you the experiences of twenty years' collecting. I take you back to a time when toys were still made with much creativity and considerable craft expertise. Perhaps you will understand that although we may be adults, the child remains with us always.

Agnes Melger

CHAPTER I

The development of the doll

The development which the doll has undergone in the course of the centuries will be outlined in this chapter. Greater strides forward were made in the development of the doll in the nineteenth century than at any other time.

History of the doll

Thousands of years before our times children must have played with dolls. The ancient Greeks and Egyptians had dolls.

The people who lived long ago in the Balkans left behind them clear indications that there were dolls then and these have since come to light through excavations. About four thousand years ago, these people made doll's houses complete with clay dolls.

In museums throughout the world today there are images to be found of people in the form of figurines that served as other than cult or sacrificial offerings, amulets, or talismans, and which were probably toys for children.

They were mainly very primitively fashioned of wood or clay. In the Middle Ages, especially within the more privileged circles, dolls were for the amusement of adults. Only in the late Middle Ages did the children of the wealthy - whether they were boys or girls – begin to play with dolls.

Composition doll, not marked, circa 1927.

Doll by Adolf Wislizenus, circa 1915, Germany.

Doll by Adolf Wislizenus, circa 1915, Germany

From about 1400, a number of craftsmen in Nuremberg carved dolls from wood. These doll-makers were called *Dockenmacher* and organized themselves in guilds. *Docke* or *Tocke* was the general term for toys at that time but in about 1700 it became used solely for dolls. The first dolls made by the members of these guilds were pin-shaped and eyes, mouths and hair were painted on.

As the demand for dolls increased, so did the quality; the pin-shaped dolls disappeared and were replaced by more life-like dolls with movable limbs attached. Through the fame of their dolls, these doll-makers were barely able to cope with the rising demand for dolls, and entire families were put to work making them. Through the increasing power of the guilds, a ban was introduced in the eighteenth century preventing unauthorized persons from making dolls and from that time only established wood-carvers and turners worked in wood to make dolls. The painting of the dolls and making of clothing for them were restricted to the guilds for painters and tailors.

The history of dolls shows us that even in the twentieth century, particularly in Germany, entire families were still employed in the making of parts for doll's bodies and the blowing of glass eyes. After 1700, the wooden dolls had rudimentary glass eyes set in and they received wigs of real hair. The scoop hands vanished and made way for fairly well shaped ones with carved fingers.

More attention was also given to the painting of the heads.

Early doll of wax over papier-mâché, not marked,
circa 1875.

The makers of composition dolls were required to adhere to very strict guild regulations, and in about 1700, it was forbidden for girls to make them. The working of wet paper or pulp was a fairly messy business and it was considered that the worthiness of a woman would be harmed by it. The dolls were constructed by a process that could be considered as a forerunner of papier-mâché. The materials used were a mixture of paper or cardboard pulp, resin, glue, and chalk that could be pressed into or imprinted with moulds when wet. The papier-mâché dolls had a more realistic appearance than their wooden counterparts.

Until about 1810, the heads of composition dolls were made by hand. Subsequently production in Germany changed over to the use

of oiled moulds. This saved considerable time so that production could be increased, resulting in cheaper mass-produced products that flooded the market. The strong battle to compete which ensued between the German and French doll industries forced the French to gather their forces together. Firms such as Bru, Jumeau, Blödel, Rabery, and Delphieu joined together in the Société Française de Fabrication des Bébés et Jouets or SFBJ, which was founded in 1899.

Wax dolls

The origins of modelling with wax lie within religion. As early as the sixteenth century, holy images and devotional figures for the Christmas crib were being made in countries such as Germany, Austria, and Spain. In some countries it was even the custom to replace a dead baby with a wax doll dressed as an infant-in-arms. This was lain in the cradle and left in the delivery room for a period of time.

In 1807, there were mask-makers in Nuremberg who also made doll's heads of wax, in addition to all kinds of wax masks. The material that they used consisted of four parts wax, three parts white turpentine, and some grease or pig's fat. To achieve the desired opacity, they were painted with vermilion or a little red lead. At the end of the nineteenth

Early doll of wax over papier-mâché, not marked,
circa 1875.

Wax doll, with box, in original condition and not marked, circa 1900.

Left: ball head of wax over papier-mâché, leather body, not marked, circa 1870.

Early wax doll with implanted hair, in original condition and not marked, circa 1870.

century kerosene or paraffin were being used to make dolls. Until 1850, the dolls were formed by hand but then wax was poured into moulds to make the heads, resulting in crisper details and more lifelike faces.

Wax dolls were also being made in Great Britain and France as well as Germany. The firms of Montanari and Pierotti of London won worldwide fame with their wax dolls.

The dolls of Augusta Montanari are of exceptional quality. Designed by her husband, the sculptor Napoleon Montanari, the dolls radiate warmth and appear so lifelike. Eyelashes, eyebrows, and hair were implanted using a heated needle pressed into the wax. The blue glass eyes and small red mouth are typical of these Montanari dolls. After the "infant-in-arms" dolls, those made by Augusta Montanari were perhaps the first baby dolls. Because of

Wax doll by Cuno & Otto Dressel, in original condition, 1885.

After the war, celluloid was gradually replaced by other plastic materials including vinyl.

There were dolls made from rigid plastic that is virtually impossible to tell apart from celluloid. In addition to this, the arms and legs were attached using old-fashioned elastic and the dolls had old-style fixed glass eyes. In view of the lack of any marking, the chance is considerable that we might buy a plastic doll in mistake for celluloid one. Only after a very thorough examination is it possible to tell the difference.

Increasing numbers of collectors intentionally seek out an attractive older celluloid doll. The days when they were considered the Cinderellas among dolls are over. Celluloid dolls play an important part in the history of dolls and they are closely bonded with the childhood of many. Few of us ever had a doll with a porcelain head because that sort of toy was too expensive and very fragile. But we were given a reasonably priced celluloid doll for our birthday or for Christmas, for which our mother or grandmother made clothes. Such dolls are to be seen for valuation at exhibitions every week on a table in front of me, lovingly cared for by their now grown-up owners, who cannot bear to part with them. These dolls should be included in every collection because it is important that they are preserved.

Ordinary old dolls

Almost all the European makers manufactured dolls from cheaper materials such as composition, in addition to the expensive bisque porcelain ones. These dolls were plainer in style and materials and were much cheaper. Composition is a combination of among other materials, plaster, glue, woodchips, and papier-mâché. Once pressed and dried, this substance is very strong and almost unbreakable.

Celluloid character doll with composition body by Kämmer & Reinhardt - Turtle mark, circa 1930, Germany.

The same moulds were often used for both composition and porcelain heads. The composition bodies vary from beautifully articulated bodies of papier-mâché to fabric bodies.

During the years of economic crisis, these dolls were very popular. Because of the enormous numbers produced and their almost indestructible material, they are now available in abundance. It is not even difficult to find a perfect example. Since the reunification of Germany, the former East Germany has opened up as a new source. Through the substantial offerings from countries such as Poland, Hungary, and the former Czechoslovakia, we tend to characterize them as ordinary cheap old dolls but this is unfair, since every doll is unique and interesting as an object to collect. There are beautiful composition dolls with very expressive faces, lovely wigs, and often still originally clad too.

Considerable numbers of these dolls were produced by the French makers such as Jumeau and subsequently SFBJ. They have considerable cultural value, bearing in mind that they were present in almost every child's room. These were true dolls to play with and not status symbols such as the porcelain dolls, which only the privileged children were given and which could only be shown off on Sundays when mother received visitors.

The earliest collections

Although the ability to own a doll was limited to the better off and especially the aristocracy of Middle Europe, there were already doll collectors in the nineteenth century.

Particularly in France, Great Britain, Germany, and the USA, dolls became very popular. Among the nobility and upper echelons, the sewing of fashionable clothes for dolls was a popular pastime for men as well as women. Doll's clubs were also founded which gave

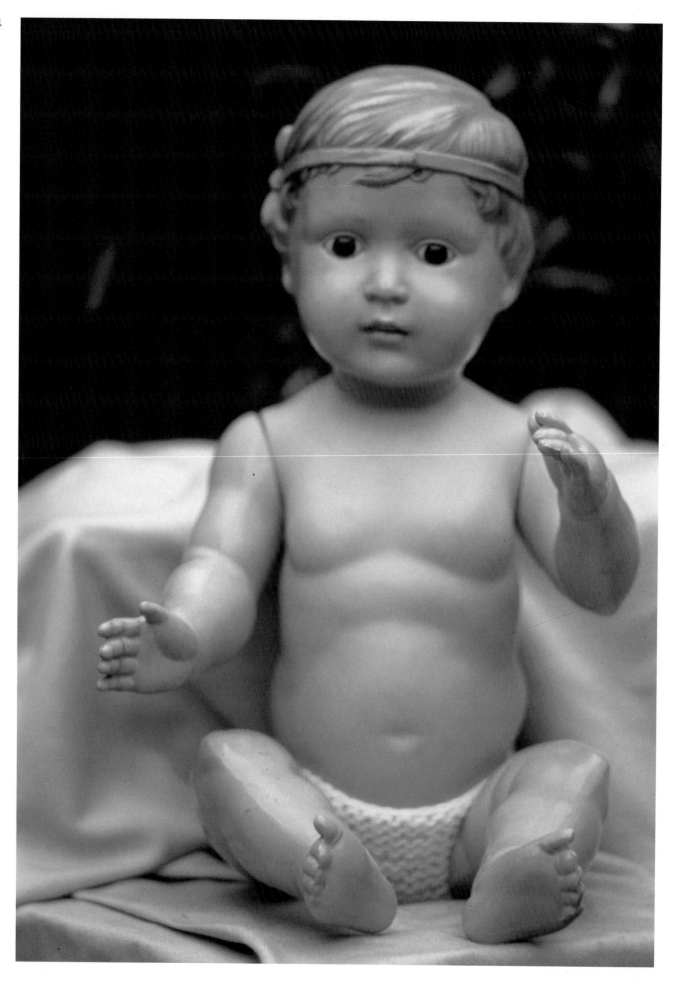

members specific projects, such as the fashion
of Maria Stuart of the French baroque period.
The winner, whose doll was perfectly dressed
with every precise historical detail, would
receive a prize or honourable mention. Many
beautiful collections came about in this way.

Left: Celluloid doll, Turtle mark, circa 1932, Germany.

Two character dolls with composition, circa 1930, Germany.

The French doll industry

The importance of the French doll industry is fully dealt with in this chapter. The French have always been among the leading doll-makers. It was they who introduced bisque heads and the so-called "paperweight" eyes. From the middle of the nineteenth century, France had a great number of doll factories which exported their bébés throughout the world, led by five top makers who each achieved world fame. Two of them battled it out continuously for the honour of best maker.

Automaton with dolls by François Gaultier,
circa 1885, France.

Léon Casimir Bru

Léon Casimir Bru, a doll-maker established in the rue Saint-Denis in Paris, applied for a patent for his dolls in 1867. He was one of the greatest competitors of Pierre François Jumeau and made dolls of outstandingly high quality. Because the production of the Bru firm was smaller than that of Jumeau, the dolls by Bru are rarer and therefore highly desired by collectors, resulting in the dolls commanding exceptional prices. Bru made finely modelled dolls with porcelain heads that could be turned. They were mounted on a shoulder plate that was also made of porcelain. The heads were almost never marked. Instead, paper labels were stuck on the body with the name and address of the maker, which dried out after a time and fell off. It is therefore very rare to see a Bru doll still bearing its label.

The early Bru dolls have a half-open mouth, delightful blue or brown hand-blown eyes - the so-called "paperweight" eyes, encircled by heavily feathered eyelashes and finely painted eyebrows. These first dolls from Casimir Bru had wigs of wool. The bodies were leather, with lower arms and lower legs of porcelain, leather, or wood.

In 1869, Léon Casimir Bru designed a body with ball joints for which he had applied for a patent. A year later, in 1870, he died and his widow Apollene Bru passed the running of the

Marotte, not marked, circa 1900.

factory to their son, Casimir Bru jr. In 1872 Apollene Bru applied for a patent in her name for a toy box, placed in a Bru doll. At this time a revolutionary change overtook the doll industry: children began to prefer dolls which looked like themselves. The manufacturers conveniently met the demand by altering the women dolls of the era into child dolls. The firm of Steiner was first on the market with a Bébé (or child doll). Jumeau followed his example in 1875 and won a gold medal or *médaille d'or* with a Bébé at the World Exhibition of 1878.

Casimir Bru recognized that he too must keep up with this development and decided in contrast to his competitors, who made composition bodies and ball-jointed limbs, to set his beautiful children's heads on leather bodies with porcelain arms and legs.

Doll by J.J. Julien, circa 1890, France

Baby doll by Unis France in original condition,
circa 1915, France.

bility. Once again Casimir Bru forged ahead of his competitors. On 3 October 1874, Casimir Bru patented an invention which was to become the company's showpiece - the Bébé Téteur (or suckling baby). The enormous success of this doll continued into the early years of the twentieth century.

The Bébé Téteur is a child doll that could drink from the baby's feeding bottle delivered with the doll, by means of a rubber bulb attached to a tube connected to the mouth. The teat of the bottle was connected to the hose in the mouth and by squeezing the bulb through an opening in the back of the head and then letting go, the doll would drink the bottle empty. By pressing the ball again, the liquid flowed back into the bottle. Unfortunately this mechanism no longer works because rubber perishes.

In 1882, Casimir Bru introduced a new wonder-child, Bébé Gourmand. This doll had the leather body of the Circle-Dot-Bru, with superbly made arms and really childlike legs of porcelain, with open-soled feet upon which were fastened shoes, the soles of which were partially removable. The name (greedy baby) comes from the doll's ability to eat small pieces of food placed in its mouth which were swallowed by a movement of the tongue so that they passed to the hollow of the doll's body and finally into its legs where the food could be removed through the opening in the

Left a Tête Jumeau and right a Eden Bébé from Fleischmann & Blödel, circa 1885-1892, France.

Subsequently he improved the bodies, giving them children's proportions. He really put much care into the porcelain arms and their fingers. His dolls, which radiated a convincing childlike appearance, surpassed everything and everyone. The Bébé Breveté (patented baby) and the Circle-Dot-Bru are highly desirable objects for every collector of antique dolls. Because the leather dolls with their rather rigid posture were less flexible than the competitors' dolls, Casimir Bru decided to change to articulated bodies and presented his new Bébé Modèle (baby model) with a very ingenious body. The body, which was completely made of wood, had arms and legs with joints and shoulders, elbows. hands, groin, knees, and, as a remarkable feature, ankle joints which gave the doll tremendous flexi-

BRU JNE
9   ⊙

BRU.JNE R
10

BRU JNE R
BREVETE S.G.D.G
Y8M

⊙; ⌒; ⊙;

⊙
BRU. JNE
13

Marks used by the Bru company.

day very closely. A Bru doll with its original clothing is a strongly coveted object by every collector.

Since no historical records appear to have been kept about the Bru company or these have been lost, many very interesting details about the company remain a mystery. We have no idea therefore why Casimir Bru some years later sold the factory to Henri Chevrot. Perhaps it was because Casimir was a man who relished new challenges and considered he had reached the limit to development in the doll industry.

Henri Chevrot continued with the factory which had become known for its quality until 1899.

Doll by Léon Casimir Bru Jne 12, circa 1885, France.

soles of the feet. In his urge for perfection, Casimir became ever more deeply involved in the development of his dolls. This resulted in 1882 in another invention: movable eyelids which closed over fixed eyes. This also meant that his production was both more difficult and increasingly more expensive.

Casimir Bru was well aware that the clothing of his dolls was a very important factor and he had very high quality hand-sewn clothes made in specially established studios which used the best fabrics and followed the fashion of the

Left: standing doll by Leon Casimir Bru Jne 12, circa 1885, sitting Tête Jumeau doll 14, circa 1890, France.

François Gaultier

Dolls by Gaultier are easily recognized by collectors. With their compact round faces with small, well-formed mouth and large hand-blown eyes, they have the somewhat strong Gaultier look. About the doll-maker himself, there is much uncertainty. In older books about antique dolls it is accepted that a Ferdinand or Fernand Gaultier started a doll factory in about 1860 in the rue Grand Hurleur in Paris. Subsequent research has shown that such a firm never existed. In 1872, the doll-maker François Gaultier applied for a patent for machines to improve the quality of porcelain doll's heads. In 1878, he received a silver medal which he renewed at exhibitions in Amsterdam (1883), Nice (1884), and Antwerp (1885).

Parisienne by François Gaultier, circa 1870, France.

Doll by François Gaultier in original condition, circa 1890, France.

During the great World Exhibition of 1889 in Paris he won a silver yet again. His greatest success was achieved with his Parisiennes which were of exceptionally fine quality.

The later dolls were of beautiful quality in the beginning with a delightful look but certain of the dolls with an open mouth from a later date that are to be found have a rather hard expression. Gaultier marked his Parisiennes with the letters FG on the back of the head and later examples have the initials FG enscrolled.
Gaultier also produced the Marottes (or dummy heads). The copies of these dolls with closed mouths, which are sometimes called "fool's baubles", were bisque heads set on a small stick of ivory or wood with a music-box mounted upon it that played one or more tunes. This luxury "rattle" played its tune as

the head turned. The clothing for the Marottes was based upon the French Mr Punch. On the head there was a fool's cap and around the neck there was a collar of satin.

The rest of the clothing consisted of a round ball of fabric to hide the music-box, and eight to ten leaf like silk or satin ribbons with jin-gling bells attached. The Marottes are interesting items for doll collectors.

In 1889, the factory was run by the two sons of François Gaultier, who made other decorative and electrical items in addition to dolls.

From 1899, the sons become members of SFBJ.

Doll by François Gaultier in original condition, circa 1890, France.

Doll by Max Handwerck, circa 1900, Germany.

Doll by Alt Beck & Gottschalck with "flirting" eyes, circa 1912, Germany.

men made their way to the town on foot, horse-back or by horse-drawn wagon on the day set for delivery by the doll-maker; this was usually a Sunday. During the winter this was a

heavy and dangerous task as their route would be heavy with snow and slippery underfoot. The completed dolls were taken by enormous wagons to the ports, for shipping all over the

Four small bisque porcelain dolls with wire bodies, not marked, Germany.

A small bisque porcelain doll, 10cm (4in) tall, circa 1912, Germany.

Doll by Heinrich Handwerck, series number 109, circa 1900, Germany.

world. The doll industry flourished as never before. A factory with an average production capacity would have at least a thousand dolls displayed in its showrooms. The social standing of the thousands of homeworkers contrasted sharply with that of the successful dollmaker. The homes of the homeworkers, in which sometimes as many as ten or more people lived, consisted of one living room which also served as the workshop and kitchen, and one bedroom without any windows, containing at least four beds. A single bed would hold two people, and a double bed would sleep four.

Houses of a similar size often had twenty to thirty people living, working, and sleeping in them during this period. In such extreme cases, the police took action and cleared the people out of the houses. A fire was kept burning in the living room the whole year so that parts of papier-mâché could dry out near the stove. The continuously high humidity in these houses was not particularly beneficial for the health of the workers or their children. Although the children would be at school for 28 hours each week, they were used as valuable additional labour in their "spare time". Their small fingers worked many hours every day, often until late into the evening. This child labour yielded between 5 and 10 Deutschmarks extra a week for the family. An unfortunate consequence was that the more children there were, the more could be earned. The family hygiene was also very difficult for them. The living room-workshop would be cleaned by the women on Saturday when the week's production was being delivered. Their clothes were also washed on the same day. Because there was usually no time left to do so, the bedroom was rarely cleaned. The children were bathed on Sunday. Their food was poor and mainly comprised potatoes. For breakfast they might eat potatoes with chicory, for the midday meal they ate potatoes, perhaps sometimes with a piece of herring, and for the evening meal it was potatoes again; sometimes, there would be bread dipped in sausage soup. Sausage soup was the water in which the butcher had cooked sausages and retained for the homeworkers. The combination of poor diet, working with clay, and the high humidity, was detrimental to their health and many developed tuberculosis.

The Sonneberg doll-makers began increasingly to concentrate on making quality dolls that were purchased by the rich. This meant that the fashions of the day had to be closely followed. A well-dressed doll changed its clothing every season. The large makers copied this idea of dressing the dolls in the latest fashions

from the French doll-makers. Every self-respecting doll-maker in Germany introduced workshops for seamstresses in which the superb doll's clothes were made. The production of the doll's clothes was as important as that of the dolls and it became another important form of employment for women and girls, freeing them from the necessity of selling their bodies. Prior to this development, the station

Doll by Andreas Müller, Sonneberg, circa 1916, Germany.

Doll by Max Handwerck, Bébé Elite, circa 1920, Germany.

Doll by Kley & Hahn, Walküre, circa 1903, Germany.

Three bisque porcelain figurines by the Heubach brothers, circa 1920, Germany.

at Sonneberg had been a busy streetwalkers' zone, because there were always passing strangers keen to make use of the services offered by the women and girls.

The Heubach brothers

It is generally known among enthusiasts that the Heubach brothers made wonderful character dolls of rare quality and beauty.

The production of these dolls did not begin until 1910, although the factory had been started in 1840.

In the intervening years, the firm had established its reputation and won one silver and three gold medals at world exhibitions in Europe and the United States with porcelain figurines that are really ornaments and with their Piano Babies. These figures have become internationally popular as collector's items.

The founder of the porcelain factory in which the Heubach brothers made history was Johann Heinrich Leder from Overlichte, who set up the factory in 1804 to make consumer goods. In 1840 the brothers Christoph and Philip Heubach from Lauscha purchased the factory and continued the production of consumer goods.

After the appointment in 1843 of Louis Heubach – Philip's son – as technical manager, the factory began to make porcelain figures,

knick-knacks, and miniatures, which were mainly exported to the United States. The firm had a close relationship with the school for sculptors in Lichte, where the factory was located. There were many talented students at this school who created many superb child figures and statues. The precise details are unknown, but the output of different subjects produced by the brothers is considerable: more than 10,000 since 1843.

Only some of them were made in bisque porcelain and these are the ones that collectors adore. The factory only acquired its first trade mark in 1882 – a setting sun. Prior to this, the figures were unmarked or had a fired-in consumer.

Bisque porcelain figurine by the Heubach brothers, circa 1920, Germany.

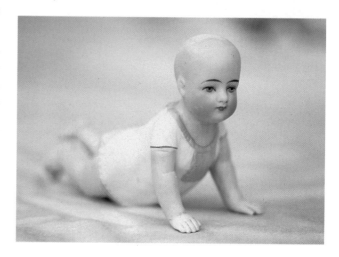

Two bisque porcelain figures by the Heubach brothers, circa 1915, Germany.

Two bisque porcelain baby figures by the Heubach brothers, circa 1920, Germany.

Louis Heubach died in 1887, one year after his son Hermann, who some years earlier had taken over the running of the factory with his two elder brothers, Philip jr. and Ottokar. These two continued with the management of the business.

Bisque porcelain baby figure by the Heubach brothers, circa 1920, Germany.

The youngest brother, who had been trained with an importer in New York, returned and joined them in the company.

At the World Exhibition in 1900, the brothers won a silver medal and four years later they won a gold medal in St Louis, and then they twice more received gold medals, in 1905 in Lüttich, and in 1906 in Milan.

The figures which were made in thousands of varieties all had one characteristic. The expression on the face is very expressive as a result of the intaglio or painted eyes with an engraved sunken iris. The hairstyles were mainly abundantly curled and the clothing of the child figures was of excellent design and colour choice.

The Heubach figures are known for the way the modelling of the clothes and hairstyle is equally detailed on the back of the figure and back of the head. The famous series of naked baby figures is irresistible. All the figures were made with an outstanding feel for quality.

Many stand, sit, or lie against a decorative background in the form of a vase-like basket, an egg, or a fine pedestal. The figures of animals which sit or stand in oversized shoes are quite unusual; the animal figures often have human expressions and they are eagerly sought. The collector should seek out examples that bear the maker's mark because many reproductions are being passed as genuine.

company celebrated its fiftieth anniversary in 1933 (which was also the year that Franz Reinhardt died) under the new management of Otto Eichhorn and Max Kritschau. The once mighty concern lost its good name as a result of general neglect and soon afterwards had to close down. The German heads had the superb "paperweight" eyes fitted to them in France.

Simon & Halbig

Carl Halbig and the toy manufacturer Wilhelm Simon founded a porcelain works in Gräfenheim, Thüringia, in 1869. This involved most of the population of the town, directly or indirectly. Carl Halbig was a caring man who

Little doll by Simon & Halbig, 1079 Dep., circa 1892, Germany.

involved himself in means to improve things for the young people of the area surrounding Gräfenheim. He built good schools, where children could get a hot meal during times of stringency. The streets of Gräfenheim had street lighting provided by him and in cold winters, all the children of the community received ice skates. The works, which began to produce doll's heads in 1870, delivered an unequalled quality. The heads, which were made at first of Parian porcelain and later of a similar fine quality bisque porcelain, were quickly known far beyond the borders of Germany. The bisque was very fine and smooth and had a good colour. In addition to this, the heads were painted with very precise attention to detail. The demand from abroad was therefore huge. Many French firms ordered the

Heinrich Handwerck – Simon & Halbig, in original condition, circa 1915, Germany.

Simon & Halbig, 1079 Dep., in original condition, circa 1892, Germany.

cheaper heads from Germany in order to compete and larger makers like Jumeau – later SFBJ – were important clients for Simon & Halbig.

Little is known about the earliest period of this firm. The first series were probably not marked in any way, or simply received a number. In 1887 the heads started to be branded with DEP on the back of the head and those for Jumeau are known by collectors as DEP-Jumeau's.

Between 1878 and 1895 – the year after Wilhelm Simon died, when Carl Halbig announced the company would continue under his management – the firm had made the 300

Upperleft: doll by Simon & Halbig – Kämmer & Reinhardt, circa 1898, Germany.

Left: doll by Simon & Halbig - Kämmer & Reinhardt, series 126, circa 1914, Germany.

Bottom: little doll by Simon & Halbig, 10cm (4in) tall, circa 1900. Little doll in a pram of German bisque porcelain, circa 1910, Germany.

and 800 series. Nothing is known about the 500 and 600 series. The 200 series is almost certainly only delivered to the Jumeau concern. From the model 728 onwards, the heads were marked according to the Simon & Halbig system. A superb example from the 700 series is model 719 DEP, that was made for Jumeau. A very expressively painted "full head" was made under the model number S13H 719DEP that had almond-shaped eyes.

In the 900 series, the models 929 and 939 are both outstanding. Number 929 has a long face, a delightfully shaped open mouth and large blue eyes and the double-jointed body has additional ball joints.

This model was also used for one of the smallest dolls made by Simon & Halbig: a model 16cm (6½in) tall, with closed mouth and a composition body with bent arms and

Doll by Simon & Halbig – Kämmer & Reinhardt, series 126, circa 1914, Germany.

Character doll by Simon & Halbig, model 127, circa 1927, Germany.

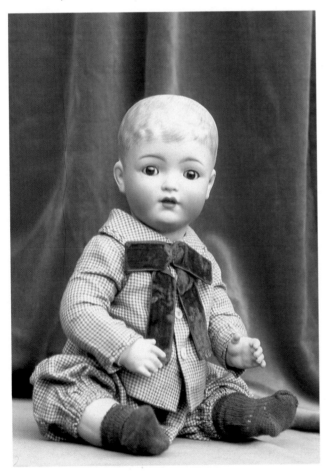

legs with knee joints. Model 939 is a wonderfully crafted head that was delivered as both an open head and as a "full head" and in both open- and closed-mouth versions. The marvellous "paperweight" eyes give the doll the appearance of a French doll; understandably this head was used by Jumeau. Collectors are also very fond of the beautiful oriental dolls – particularly those from the 1100, 1200, and 1300 series.

The doll's house dolls that Simon & Halbig made wholly of porcelain, in sizes between 7.5 and 18cm (3 and 7in), are of the same wonderful quality and have enormous expressive faces with either fixed or sleeping eyes, and open or closed mouths, with fine wigs, and superb clothing.

The shoes and stockings were painted on to the legs. The firm also made oriental dolls in these sizes.

The works were bought by Kämmer & Reinhardt and the combined businesses achieved worldwide renown with the excellent character series that were marked with S & H and K & R, which are highly sought after by collectors of dolls. In 1919 the firm celebrated its fiftieth anniversary and Carl Halbig his eighteenth birthday. It was this year too when Carl passed the management of the company over to his son Arno, who died in 1926. Three years after his son's death, the founder of the business died, aged 87.

CHAPTER 4

Two famous doll-makers

Two women were of inestimable value for the doll industry and they awakened motherly feelings in countless children with their delightful fabric dolls: the German Käthe Kruse and the Italian Elena Scavini – better known as Madame Lenci.

Doll by Käthe Kruse, model 1, circa 1920, Germany.

Right: Käthe Kruse, dolls IH and 10, circa 1930, and doll I, circa 1940, Germany.

Käthe Kruse

Käthe Kruse was born Katharina Simon in Breslau on 17 September 1883. Once she left school, Käthe wanted to be an actress and took acting lessons. A combination of talent and determination won her a contract a year later paying 250 Deutschmarks with the Mark & Lessing theatre in Berlin. When she was 19, she got to know the artist Max Kruse, who was thirty years older than her. Käthe wanted to have children with Max but did not want to get married. Their relationship resulted in the birth of their first daughter, Maria Speranza (Mimerle), causing Käthe to quit the acting profession. A second daughter, Fifi was born the following year. When Mimerle asked for a doll for Christmas in 1905, Käthe looked one with a porcelain head. Max did not approve, saying that the hard, rigid heads did not stir motherly feelings in a child. He suggested that Käthe make a doll herself. Käthe considered Max's advice and then made her first doll: a glove filled with warm sand, with knots to create arms and legs. A large potato was bound in fabric to act as the head and the eyes, nostrils, and mouth were drawn in using used matches. It was certainly no work of art but Mimerle was enchanted with it. This was only the first of many dolls and the Kruse family grew. A third daughter – Joanna Irmfriede Ceres (Hannerle) – was born in 1909, and in March that same year Käthe and Max married after all.

During a visit to Munich, Käthe found a "Fiamingo" head that was a reproduction of a child's head by the Flemish baroque sculptor

Weighted "sand" baby by Käthe Kruse, circa 1928, Germany.

Weighted "sand" baby by Käthe Kruse, circa 1928, Germany.

Above: Käthe Kruse (from left to right) – doll 1, circa 1916, Bambino, circa 1923, and doll 1, circa 1916, Germany.

Left: Hanne Kruse, Däumlinchen (Jockerle) 25cm (10in) tall, 1965, Germany.

The dolls of Käthe Kruse

The most admired collector's pieces are the so-called "bareheads", with a head made of impregnated fabric which is then hand-painted with oil paints and is hand-sewn to a very realistic child's body. The legs, with five seams are attached to broad hips with a disc joint. The so-called "frog's hands" are cut from one piece and the doll, which was made until 1912, is filled with reindeer hair.

In 1913 the doll's hands changed style; the fingers were stitched through and a separate thumb was sown on. This doll was always described as doll 1 and continued to be shown in the catalogue until 1922.

The signature of Käthe is under the left foot of

the doll and under the right foot there is a stamp with the serial number.

This model 1 doll is 43cm (17in) tall and it remained in production until 1933. In 1934 the doll was changed to a simpler cutting pattern. The hips and legs became smaller and the doll grew 2cm (3/4in) taller to 45cm (17 3/4in). The catalogue gave an incorrect height of 43cm (17in) until 1949. This doll continued in production until 1951.

Schlenkerchen, a stockinette doll from 1922 with a laughing face, is 33cm (13in) tall, has supple legs, and was indicated as doll 2 in the catalogue. Later dolls were made in various sizes and had wigs. Käthe's first baby doll, which was used to train midwives, had closed eyes. The body of this doll had a navel sewn on and was weighted with sand to 2.25kg (5lb). This "sand baby", called Träumerchen, which is now an eagerly sought after collector's piece, was made in two versions: one of 2.25kg (5lb) and 50cm (19 3/4in) length and the other weighing 2.75kg (6lb) and 60cm (23 1/2in) long. An unweighted doll with open eyes was also made called Du Mein.

The weighted Träumerchen is often incorrectly called Du Mein. Both the Deutsches Kind and Hampelchen dolls are very popular with collectors. The latter doll is 45cm (17 3/4in) tall and appears in the 1931 catalogue under the name of Notstandskind. The model for the head was made by Igor Jakimow. The body has a pair of supple legs that can be fixed with a ribbon to the back by a button fastener.

The doll's clothes were initially designed by Käthe herself but eventually this was taken over by Anne Kurreck. Standards were high for both the materials and the quality of the doll's clothes. Käthe wanted superb clothes in cheerful colours and her preference for red is

Käthe Kruse, doll 1, circa 1925, and doll 1H, circa 1929, Germany.

Right: Käthe Kruse, Friedebald, circa 1929, and Annemarie, circa 1932.

Top: Käthe Kruse, doll 1, 1915, doll 1, circa 1913, and soldiers, circa 1915-1918, Germany.

Right: Ilsebell and Friedebald, circa 1930, by Käthe Kruse, Germany.

Lower right: Käthe Kruse doll 7, circa 1931, and Hampelchen, circa 1949, Germany.

quite obvious. In 1928, Käthe began to design Sunday outfits for the dolls using, until 1939, expensive fabrics like silk, cambric, chiffon, and organza.

The shoes were designed to match the clothes. From 1950, when Käthe had abandoned Kössen, the shoes were marked on using pencils and from 1954, when the business became part of the State concern VEB, the dolls were stamped with a triangle and/or "VEB Bad Kössen a.d. Saale", occasionally with the addition of "Rat des Kreises Naumburg/Saal".

Although these dolls no longer bore the Käthe Kruse name, they were sold in some shops as Kruse dolls. These VEB dolls are easily recognized. Their cutting is much simpler, the fabric is different, and the seam at the back of the knee is missing. The expressionless eyes and painting of the dolls give a rather cool appearance. In 1955 the dolls were given plastic heads. The Schildkrot (Turtle) firm started to make Käthe Kruse dolls in 1955, which were given both the Turtle mark and the name of Käthe Kruse.

Madame Lenci

The Italian Elena Scavini is better known as Madame Lenci, world-renowned for her felt dolls. In common with her German counterpart Käthe Kruse, Madame Lenci made fabric dolls. In contrast with the Käthe Kruse dolls though, which are a bit serious and look

somewhat puzzled, the Lenci dolls look relaxed and untroubled and just a bit cheeky. One thing that the two women had in common as doll-makers is that they both began making them as a hobby and they both continually sought to achieve artistic perfection. The dolls of Madame Lenci, which look out on the world rather saucily – mainly from right to left – are not yet well known to collectors. These dolls, which have two fingers joined together, are wonderfully dressed in costumes of felt and organza.

There are various stories told about Madame Lenci. At the end of the First World War she lived with her husband in Turin, where the main employment was in the garment industry. According to one story she was widowed during the First World War and began making dolls as a solace from her grief. Another story says that she decided to make dolls for other children after the loss of her only child. With a third story, her husband Enrico was so badly wounded in the war that he could not work and they decided that she should make money from her talent. The second story is perhaps the most likely.

The first dolls were known under the name of Scavini. The brand name Lenci was derived from the pet name by which Enrico called Elena. The dolls were registered in Italy and Great Britain under the name Lenci di E. Scavini and in 1924 were registered in the United States under the name Lenci, with the remark that the name Lenci was already used since February 1920. The trading lists in the United States contain details of dolls, mannequin dolls, figures, animal figures, character dolls, toys, and wheels. The branding was stamped on the dolls, the packaging, and there were also paper labels. Sometimes there were even marks woven into the clothing. In 1920, the

Doll 9 by Käthe Kruse, circa 1930, and Friedebald, circa 1930, Germany.

time. The company exhibited them throughout the world at all the most important exhibitions.

Many other well-known French makers produced coloured dolls, such as Daniel et Cie, Denamur, SFBJ, and Unis France. In addition to bisque porcelain, they also used other materials to make the brown and black dolls. Many coloured dolls are still to be seen which were made of composition, and many coloured dolls were also made of celluloid. Makers such as Lenci, who made felt dolls, and Chad Valley, who produced fabric dolls, also joined in with coloured dolls in their range.

When I remarked that not all coloured dolls possess realistic negro or oriental features, I did not of course mean that they are not worth collecting. My comment was merely intended to illustrate the fact that certain makers set different creative standards for their modellers.

Left: two oriental dolls by Ernst Heubach, model 452, circa 1928, Germany.

Below: two oriental dolls by Ernst Heubach, models 414 and 399, circa 1925-30, Germany.

Parisiennes

Anyone who is able to visit the Musée National in Monaco will agree that there are few dolls that can compete with the Parisiennes in terms of quality and beauty. The fine period villa contains an impressive collection of these dolls set out in many display cases on the first floor, complete with every imaginable accessory, all collected during her life by Madame Madeleine de Galea (1874–1956).

She bequeathed her collection to the small nation on the Mediterranean in which she spent her later years.

The Parisiennes were made in both France and Germany between 1860 and 1890. These miniature adults were never intended in the first instance as toys but as amusement for ladies "from the better circles". Although some German makers produced superb examples, the French Parisiennes are in a class of their own. The delicate, almost transparent white bisque porcelain heads, which are either fixed or movable, upon similar bisque porcelain shoulder pieces, have finely modelled faces, with large hand-blown "paperweight" eyes, with radiant irises.

The painting of the eyebrows, eyelashes, and mouth was very skilled and precise in detail. The fine wigs were works of art in themselves. The earliest Parisiennes have bodies of very fine leather, accentuating the femininity with a very slender waist and broad hips. Elbows, groin, and knees were notched so that the

Doll's boots, circa 1880, France.

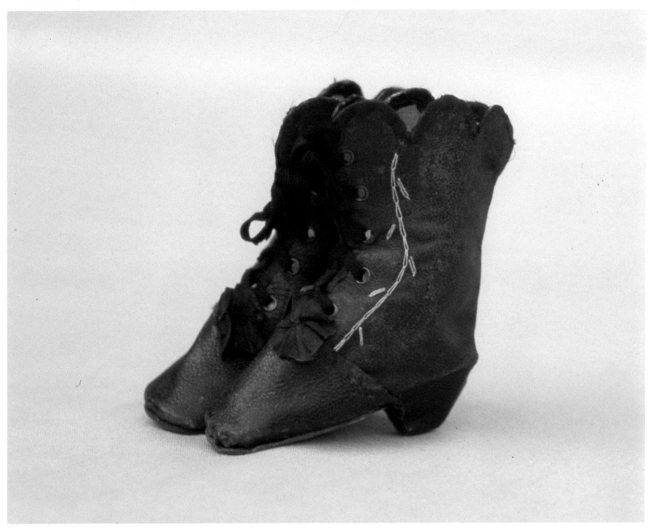

Parisienne with shoulder-head and leather body, not marked,
circa 1865, France.

François Gaultier Parisienne, circa 1870, France.

dolls could sit. Bodies made of fabric were also used, with porcelain forearms and legs. This
was followed by the better quality dolls with
wooden bodies, double articulated with movable hands. These early Parisiennes also had
rounded faces. After 1870, the faces become
smaller and more elongated.

If the makers marked their Parisiennes, this
was usually in the form of a stamp or a metal
plate with the name and address of the maker,
which was generally located on the front of
the doll's body. Signatures are rarely found on
the porcelain heads, but if there is any mark, it
will most likely be a number. The majority of
Parisiennes are unmarked so that it is essential
to look for characteristic signs that are recog-
nizable as the work of a particular maker, in
order to be able to determine who made a

specific doll. This is not a simple business and
it requires considerable knowledge and experi-
ence.

The most eagerly sought collector's pieces are
the dolls with an enigmatic smile, that are
often known as the Mona Lisa Parisiennes.

Most of the French Parisiennes have a cork
covering for the top of the head to which the
wig is attached.

Another name for the Parisiennes is Lady Doll
or mannequin. These dolls were dressed according to the latest fashion and they were
used by the major fashion houses in Paris and
London to show off the latest creations to
their clientele. These fashion dolls were sub-
ject to privileged status granted to them by the
authorities so that they could be freely exported, even at times of discord between

Parisienne with shoulder-head on a leather body, not marked, circa 1865, France.

Parisienne by François Gaultier, in original condition, circa 1870, France.

France and Great Britain. Clubs were established in both Paris and London where members met to make and exchange clothes for the dolls. It was only towards the end of the nineteenth century when greater consideration started to be given to children that some Parisiennes were given to children – albeit those from the better off families.

These dolls were sold with and without clothing. The dressed dolls came complete with a case full of clothing containing an entire outfit with abundant accessories.

These included very fine underwear, nightdresses, very luxurious outer clothes, boots, bags, parasols, hats, and jewellery; there would even be opera glasses and *face-à-main* – a pair of spectacles mounted on a handle. When the doll was sold without clothes, the

doll's owner would make a complete outfit – perhaps with the mother's or governess's help. There were even magazines specially for children such as La Poupée Modèle (The Model Doll) and *Gazette de la Poupée* (The Doll's Gazette). Both of these publications carried patterns for making doll's clothes, hats, and accessories, together with news about dolls and educational advice for the young owners of dolls. Many of the doll-makers that made Parisiennes were run by women with an eye for fashion: Mesdames Rohmer and Simonne, and Mesdemoiselles Huret, Peronne, and Bereux. These women did not just make the dolls, they also sold – for high prices – the most beautiful clothes and accessories, which they had made for them by homeworkers who earned less than 50 centimes a day. Other famous makers of Parisiennes included Bru, Jumeau, Gaultier, and Barrois, who all sold doll's clothes in addition to the dolls.

The German makers of Lady Dolls included such important names as Simon & Halbig, Kestner, and Alt Beck & Gottschalck.

Boudoir or sofa dolls

There is very little written about boudoir or sofa dolls. Perhaps this is because they were never intended to be children's toys. They deserve much greater consideration that has been given to them to date. These dolls are such expressive, elegant, lady-like dolls dressed in the fashion of their time, and were an important form of interior decorative object in

the 1920s and 1930s. During the 1960s and 1970s these dolls were widely available and could be bought at shows and from market stalls for quite reasonable prices – especially in Belgium and France. Unfortunately most of them were in poor condition, with patchy and damaged faces, and usually with broken arms and legs. This is not very surprising since the dolls are very delicate objects. The heads were made of fabric. Fine linen gauze was covered with flesh-coloured material which was then painted – or some say "made up". Some boudoir dolls have eyelashes of real hair stuck on. The mouths are normally nicely shaped and painted in brilliant red. The doll's hair is of silk or mohair and was created in the style of the time. The shoulder-heads are sewn or

Parisienne by François Gaultier, in original condition, circa 1865, France.

Three boudoir dolls in original condition, circa 1925-1930, France.

Marks used for Parisienne dolls

glued to fabric bodies, that are mostly stuffed with cotton wool; the limbs are usually of composition.

The forearms are normally complete with prettily shaped hands with red varnished fingernails and the long slim lower legs tend to have golden high-heeled shoes on the feet. Boudoir dolls were also made with wax heads or even entirely of composition. They might also have glass eyes, such as the dolls by Herman Steiner. There are also, but much more rarely, male boudoir dolls.

Many designers in Europe designed boudoir dolls but the majority of these dolls were made in France or the United States. Because boudoir dolls were rarely marked, it is very difficult to determine their makers. These dolls were also known as Flapper dolls, French dolls, and Bed dolls.

Dolls were modelled upon glamorous women such as Marlene Dietrich, Josephine Baker, and Joan Crawford. These dolls, which were principally decorative items, became eagerly collected at the time they were being made – the famous Russian soprano, Lillian Lipkowska had an impressive collection of them. The dolls were always superbly dressed in the finest quality clothing. Considerable attention to detail was given in particular to the female dolls to ensure they were in the latest style.

Materials such as taffeta silk, lace, brocade, and fur were used and there was no scrimping on the quantity either to ensure the clothes were as fine as possible. It is rare to find underclothes for these boudoir dolls because the garments were normally sewn to the bodies. It was therefore impossible to undress these dolls. Consequently most dolls are still to be found with their original clothing.

The *Ladies' Home Journal* of December 1924 contained a competition for its readers in which they were to make a French Cloth Doll from 61cm (2ft) of fabric after the style of a famous person from the times when crinolines were worn. The magazine recommended the use of materials such as silk, velvet, fur, and gold and silver brocade for the costumes.

Since boudoir dolls were not produced in large quantities, it is rare to come across two identical examples. The fun of collecting these dolls is in the quest for a perfect specimen.

Boudoir doll in original condition, circa 1925, France.

Finding such an undamaged dolls is unfortunately very rare. The boudoir dolls that are available have usually had at least 60 years' exposure to light, dust, and damp, that have usually spoiled the fabric. There is little point in trying to remove brown stains caused by dampness, since this will not be successful and simply cause further stains and rings.

The clothes are often stained and torn and look shabby. Those who decide to collect these dolls in spite of the risks attached, need to keep a critical eye open. It is acceptable for a doll with a fabric head to be a little dirty but it must have a good appearance. The painting of the face and mouth in particular should not be damaged, and noses, chins and cheeks which have been pushed in are ugly.

Slight damage to an arm or leg is not too serious but if fingers or a foot is missing that is serious damage. It is not a problem if the clothing is a little faded provided that there is not too much damage showing. Check too that the wig is still in reasonable condition. The price to be paid for a boudoir doll is highly dependent upon its condition, but it should not be too high.

Boudoir doll in original condition, circa 1930, France.

Boudoir doll in original condition, circa 1930, France.

CHAPTER 6

Maintaining and valuing antique dolls

Collecting old and antique dolls is a costly affair. The interest in such dolls has grown steadily since the 1920s so that in our present times the prices have risen considerably. In this chapter you will learn how to assess the value of antique dolls, and how to take care of them to preserve their value.

Restoration of a celluloid doll by Turtle.

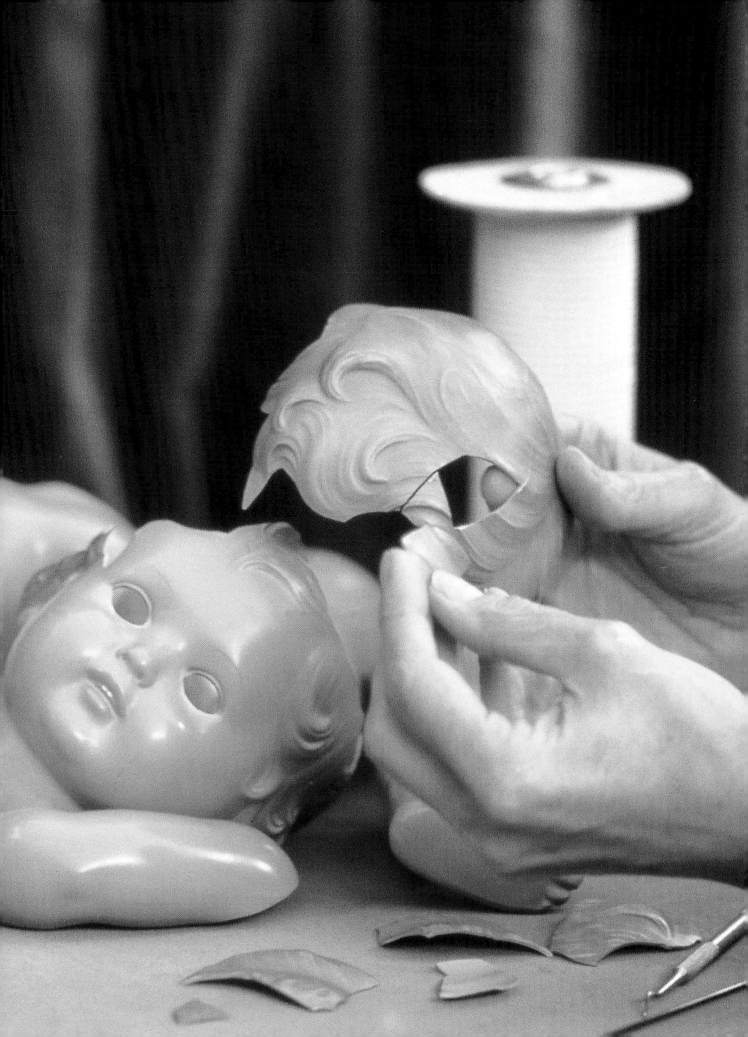

Cleaning dolls

Some collectors like old and antique dolls to look unkempt but I prefer them to look cared for, and therefore I clean them very carefully. For porcelain heads, I use some cotton wool dipped in lukewarm soapy water. The glass eyes tend to get dirty in their corners and for these I use cotton buds. For the wigs, which can become sticky to the touch, I separate the hairs with my fingers so that the hair falls more naturally loose; do not brush or comb the wigs or the hair is liable to fall out. The bodies are best cleaned using a dry cloth because they are almost always made of materials which can be damaged by becoming wet.

The clothing is washed by hand in a solution of soft soap and then well rinsed with lukewarm water and pressed dry in a towel.

Delicate fabrics such as old silk and lace are best allowed to dry flat. Cotton, linen, and other stronger fabrics can be hung up to dry but should never be tumble-dried. Press the clothes with a cool iron and, if desired, starch cotton clothing lightly so that it is more dirt-resistant. You will be dumbfounded by how such care improves the appearance.

Make it a habit to clean your dolls once a year; if they are kept in a showcase, once every two years should suffice. A stoneware head should never be cleaned with water because the colour is applied after the earthenware is fired and not fire-glazed as with porcelain. For celluloid heads it is best to use a gentle cleaning agent such as a soft soap, but never use any synthetic substances. Metal heads should be cleaned with a soft dry cloth and dolls which are entirely stuffed have to be cleaned with a soft brush because any water would leave unsightly patches. Papier-mâché dolls are very easily spoiled, so since a fingerprint can easily leave a mark, it is best to leave them alone.

Composition is fairly robust and can be wiped over with a damp cloth. Do not press too hard, because the paint can easily be removed. Handle rubber dolls with the utmost care, otherwise there is unlikely to be much left of them. The material is so soft and eventually perishes, so that it turns easily to granular form. They are best kept in a cool, damp place,

Little head of bisque porcelain, not marked, circa 1900.

Child's mittens with doll's head of papier-mâché, circa 1925, probably French.

Doll by Moa, with shoulder-head on a leather body, circa 1900, Austria.

Little doll of Parian porcelain, in original condition, not marked, circa 1900.

and coated with talcum or magnesium powder two to three times each year. My two superb rubber dolls by Hümmel disintegrated after six years in spite of the great care I took of them.

Dolls of fabric and felt

Insects and their larvae can live in dolls made of fabric, including felt, and these can also spoil the clothing. It is advisable to treat these dolls twice each year with substances that will kill the insects. The local authority may be able to advise of a place where they can be treated in a vacuum chamber to get rid of unwanted occupants. This can also be done by removing any metal parts and jewellery from the doll before placing it in the freezer, lying flat in a freezer bag with as much air as possible expelled. Leave the doll for 48 hours,

then remove and open the bag, but leave the doll to defrost for a further 48 hours.

Wax dolls

The cleaning of wax dolls is best left to a good restorer. How well the doll retains its condition depends very much on the quality of the wax used. The earlier wax dolls in particular, which were often made from one solid piece of wax, have remained in good condition provided they have been kept in their special wooden boxes or under glass.

The wrong temperature or exposure to light can be harmful for a doll. If the doll becomes too warm, the wax may dry out, causing it to crack; this is especially true of wax over papier-mâché, when such cracks can spoil the face. Cracking of the wax can even lead to

cracks, crazing, or unevenness in the earthen-ware. The lamp inside the head will also let you see if the head has been previously restored. It is difficult to shine the light through the area surrounding the eyes because the eyes are fixed in place with plaster. Check this area very carefully, using a loupe (jeweller's magnifying glass) if necessary, to make sure there are no cracks in the corners of the eye sockets and that they have not been pushed in. Check the setting of the eyes themselves to ensure that they are sound and that they correctly fit the eye socket. With a doll that has sleeping or flirting eyes, make sure that they still work

properly. If the doll has an open mouth, there should be porcelain teeth. Some character dolls and bébés also have a tongue and in some cases this is also movable. The "full head" dolls without a hole in the head, that are mounted on shoulders, can only have a light shone through them by removing the head from the shoulders.

When you have shone the light through the head, carefully pull the head away from the body and check the underside of the neck which is located in the body for any damage. It often happened that the heads did not come out of the moulds too easily – those with serious flaws were thrown away, but those with minor flaws, such as holes in the ear lobes, were not readily discarded. Flaws around the eyes, nose, or mouth are considered as serious

Left: little doll by Chad Valley, Norah Wellings, circa 1935, Great Britain.

Below: two character baby dolls by A.G. Limbach, model 8682, in original condition, 1911, Germany.

Two Martha Chase dolls, circa 1922, USA.

Early doll by J.D Kestner with shoulder-head, circa 1890, Germany.

Biscuit porcelain head on a mohair body, circa 1923, Germany.

Left: Princess Elizabeth doll, Schoenau & Hoffmeister – Porzellanfabrik Burggrub, 1929, Germany.

Following pages: six little dolls, 8cm (3½ in) tall, by J.D. Kestner, in original condition, circa 1910, Germany.

defects, together with any discolouring of the porcelain on the doll's face.

The bodies were of very variable quality and made of papier-mâché, composition, or wood, sometimes with ball joints which should still move properly. The elastic which holds the head in place should not have lost its tension. Because the bodies cannot be readily cleaned due to their being made of materials that are easily damaged by water, they usually look far less attractive than the porcelain head.

Sometimes the doll's body will seem grubbier than usual because it has been played with extensively. The undressing and dressing of the doll may have led to the loss or damage of fingers, legs, and feet. Dolls that have not been played with and therefore have perfect bodies are so rare that some collectors do not object to the odd missing finger, provided the damage is limited.

After you have checked the head and the body, check that the marks on the doll accord with the maker that the person offering the doll for sale has stated.

It is often possible to find old dolls at markets and exhibitions that are just a collection of spare parts in a box or bag, or with which the limbs hang sadly loose, eyes rattle loosely in the head, with half-missing wigs or none at all, and with cracked heads or with pieces that

have fallen out. Such hopeless cases can be re-stored with the necessary love, knowledge, and patience.

An advantage of such examples is that they should not cost very much.

Miniature doll of German bisque porcelain, 5cm (2in) tall, not marked, circa 1910.

Below: little doll of Parian porcelain, in original condition, not marked, circa 1880.

Right: doll by J.D. Kestner, model 171, in original condition, circa 1911, Germany.

Two miniature porcelain dolls, 3cm (1 1/4 in) and 8cm (3 1/4 in) tall, not marked, circa 1920.

Two miniature German dolls, 8cm (3 1/4 in) tall, in original condition, circa 1915.

Three miniature bisque porcelain dolls, not marked, circa 1915.

Forgeries

Unfortunately, forgeries of antique dolls are made, and increasingly so since in recent years the popularity and therefore the value of them has risen sharply, while the supply of genuine dolls has dwindled. The demand is considerable throughout the entire world for early bisque porcelain dolls with closed mouths by the famous French doll-makers.

Reproductions which are clearly marked as such are a different matter but very clever forgeries appear with monotonous regularity from the United States, Japan, and even France. These are so good that everything appears to be right to the eye. They are made from superb quality porcelain and have the correct "paperweight" eyes, with perfectly painted mouths, eyebrows and eyelashes. If such a forged head is mounted on an old body, with a old wig, it is very hard to tell it apart from the original.

Such dolls are offered for sale at auction for astronomical sums and it can be very difficult to spot them as forgeries.

The run of the mill forgery will be spotted by any collector with a reasonable level of knowledge but this is much more difficult with a really clever one. In the twenty odd years that I have been collecting, I have encountered good and rather less good forgeries. I tend to rely heavily upon my instincts – if I have any doubts, then I will not buy the doll. Naturally I am alerted if a very rare type of doll is being regularly offered for sale. In such cases, extreme caution is required because there is a strong possibility that forgeries are involved.

Make sure that you always purchase from trusted sources and insist upon a sales guarantee. A reliable seller will be happy to provide one. Certificates of authenticity are a figment

Doll by Schoenau & Hoffmeister, circa 1906, Germany.

Below: two character dolls by Bäehr & Prœschild, model 585, circa 1912, Germany.